Alfred Noble Library
32901 Plymouth Road
Livonia, MI 48150-1793
(734) 421-6600

J629.222
A

Things I Like

I Like Cars

Livonia Public Library
ALFRED NOBLE BRANCH
32901 PLYMOUTH ROAD
Livonia, Michigan 48150-1793
(734)421-6600
LIVN #19

Angela Aylmore

Heinemann Library
Chicago, Illinois

NOV -2 2007

© 2007 Heinemann Library
a division of Reed Elsevier Inc.
Chicago, Illinois

Customer Service   888–454–2279
Visit our website at www.heinemannlibrary.com

All rights reserved. No part of this publication may be reproduced or transmitted in any form or by any means, electronic or mechanical, including photocopying, recording, taping, or any information storage and retrieval system, without permission in writing from the publisher.

Photo research by Erica Newbery
Designed by Joanna Hinton-Malivoire
Printed in China by South China Printing Company Limited

11 10 09 08 07
10 9 8 7 6 5 4 3 2 1

Library of Congress Cataloging-in-Publication Data
Aylmore, Angela.
  I like cars / Angela Aylmore.
      p. cm. -- (Things I like)
  Includes bibliographical references and index.
  ISBN-13: 978-1-4034-9268-5 (library binding-hardcover)
  ISBN-10: 1-4034-9268-9 (library binding-hardcover)
  ISBN-13: 978-1-4034-9277-7 (pbk.)
  ISBN-10: 1-4034-9277-8 (pbk.)
  1. Automobiles--Juvenile literature. I. Title.
  TL147.A95 2007
  629.222--dc22
                                        2006024839

Acknowledgments
The publishers would like to thank the following for permission to reproduce photographs: Alamy pp. **10** (Mark Scheuer), **16** (Bananastock), **22** (Model T Ford, Mark Scheuern); Alvey & Towers pp. **6**, **22**; Auto-Express p. **8**; Corbis pp. **7** (Alan Schein Photography), **9** (Schlegelmilch Photography), **11** (Bettmann), **12** (Bettmann), **14**, **20–21** (MGM), **22**; Jupiter Images pp. **15** (Bananastock), **17** (Bananastock); Digital Vision pp. **4–5** (red car); Photos.com pp. **4–5** (all except red and racing car); Photolink pp. **4–5** (racing car); REX Features p. **19** (Tim Rooke); Science Photo Library pp. **18** (Keith Kent), **22** (Keith Kent); Science Museum p. **13** (Science and Society).

Cover photograph of a sports car reproduced with permission of Getty Images (Neil Nissing/Taxi).

Every effort has been made to contact copyright holders of any material reproduced in this book. Any omissions will be rectified in subsequent printings if notice is given to the publisher.

3 9082 10533 1956

Contents

Some words are shown in bold, **like this**. You can find out what they mean by looking in the Glossary.

Cars

I like cars.

I will tell you my favorite things about cars.

Different Cars

This car is very small.

This car is so big that my whole class could fit inside it.

These cars can drive
through water.

This car is my favorite.
It is a racing car. It is
very fast.

Old Cars

I like old cars, too. I have seen a lot of old cars at a car **museum**.

This was one of the
first cars ever.

You had to wind this car up with a handle.

The first cars were very slow. You could run faster than this old car.

Taking Care of Cars

I like helping my dad take care of his car. We wash it to keep it clean.

We go to the **gas** station.
Mom fills the car with gas.

Sometimes, mom puts air in the **tires**.

Once our car **broke down.**
We took it to a garage to
be **repaired.**

Famous Cars

I like famous cars. This is
the fastest car in the world.
It is called the Thrust SSC.

This is Batman's car. It is from a movie. I wonder what it is like to ride inside?

This is another famous car. It is called Chitty Chitty Bang Bang.

This car is the star of a movie.

Do You Like Cars?

Now you know why I like cars! Do you like cars, too?

Glossary

break down when something stops working

gas fuel for engines

museum place where interesting objects are displayed for people to look at

repair to fix something

tires rubber rings filled with air that cover wheels and help them grip the road

23

Find Out More

Mayer, Cassie. *By Car.*
  Chicago: Heinemann Library, 2006.

Miller, Heather. *Cars.*
  Chicago: Heinemann Library, 2003.

Piehl, Janet. *Formula One Race Cars.*
  Minneapolis, Minn.: Lerner, 2004.

Index